GREAT RECOVERY
QUOTES & STORIES
to Inspire
GREAT HEALERS

Noah benShea

Publisher: Foundations Recovery Network
        5409 Maryland Way, Ste. 320
        Brentwood, TN 37027

21 20 19 18 17 16   1 2 3 4 5

ISBN: 978-0-9978543-1-2
Author photo taken by Jordan benShea/skyviewprojects.com. Used with permission.

Every attempt has been made to contact copyright holders. If copyright holders have not been properly acknowledge, please contact us. Foundations Recovery Network will be happy to rectify the omission in future printings of the book.

Cover design and art by Jonny Stovall. Interior design by Sara Streifel, Think Creative Design.

Thank You

Foundations Recovery Network

Heroes in Recovery

Rob Waggener

Lee Pepper

Anna McKenzie

Wendy Lee Nentwig

Patrick Hughes

and

You

This book is dedicated to all the healers

Who by their work in the field of recovery

Make a profound difference

In a profoundly indifferent world.

Thank you.

Although the world is full of suffering,
it is also full of the overcoming of it.

Helen Keller

To be a healer is sacred work.

And like all sacred work

It requires the healer to take their work seriously

But not themselves.

Noah benShea

YES, YOU CAN

YES, YOU WILL!

Dear Healer,

I have on many occasions in my life been introduced as a poet and philosopher. But as the author and editor of this book I come to you simply as a truth teller. So, here is the truth: We all have the capacity to be healing, and we are all—at some point—in need of healing. Certainly we all discover that strength isn't the absence of weakness but how we wrestle with our weaknesses.

In this book you will find quotes and stories of wisdom, compassion, and strengthening. Rest assured, if I could have put before you better ideas more briefly said, I would have.

But, wherever you are at this moment in your life and in your good work, I ask you to take these three truths to heart and be heart healing:

1. We are all alone, but we are all alone together.

2. There is no shame in being ill; there is shame in shaming others for being ill.

3. There is courage in healing.

Some may deny these truths or because of their own failings choose to scapegoat others, but those whose contribution is condemnation are wrong—even if they are wrong with conviction. All information we learn is not equal. That people once thought the world was flat did not mean that Columbus sailed over the edge. So sail on, recovery is the discovery within.

Of course, there is no magic in any recovery. It is hard work. But in this brief life we repeatedly discover that success is often buried in hard work. Hopefully you love—or will learn to love—yourself enough to make your work a labor of love.

May each of you reading these words go from strength to strength and be a source of strength to others.

And on your journey, may you discover my smile on your shoulder and this cheer in your ear singing loudly: "Yes, you can. Yes, you will!"

Blessings.

Noah benShea

Table of Contents

Chapter One

WE ARE ALL HEALING

When I stand before thee at the day's end,
thou shalt see my scars and know
that I had my wounds and also my healing.

Rabindranath Tagore

Our sorrows and wounds are healed only
when we touch them with compassion.

Buddha

Chapter Two

COURAGE

*For me to tell my story
and give others courage,
that's my calling.*

Matthew Read

I fought addiction all my life. While I was introduced to my twelve-step fellowship in 1986, those meetings only planted a seed. My road to recovery would be a long one, marked by seven rehabs, bankruptcy, and lost cars and homes. It wouldn't be until July of 2010, when I was in my mid-fifties that treatment would finally stick.

I grew up in the '70s, and my drug of choice was amphetamines—crank or crystal meth as it's known today. It almost destroyed me before I reached out for help one last time. I can still remember the fireworks that were going off as I came down from a three- or four-day meth binge and hadn't called my partner in several days. I turned around and looked at my little parakeet and said, "Gracie, I can't even take care of you."

My quick fixes weren't working anymore. I was doing the same thing and expecting different results, and I knew if something didn't change, I was going to die. I headed to inpatient treatment at Michael's House in Palm Springs and stayed for forty-five days, dealing with a lot of issues I'd never really dealt with before. And there was plenty to deal with.

I was adopted when I was three months old and struggled with abandonment issues. In my adoptive home, my sister was deaf and that disability often took center stage. Then, when I was sixteen, I was tied to a bed and repeatedly raped. An early marriage to a woman, despite being unsure if I was bisexual or gay, added to my list of issues.

I pushed so many things down. I didn't really understand the repercussions of guilt and shame, and I was definitely not in touch with the trauma I'd gone through. What I learned in treatment was that until I reach in and pull that out, I'll just keep doing the same thing over and over.

Once I had some time in recovery under my belt, I knew it was time to give back. One thing you hear again and again from those on this journey is you can't keep anything unless you give it away. And you quickly find that when you begin to give of yourself, it comes back to you.

For me, to tell my story and give others hope, that's my calling.

It's easy to be overcome by regrets. *Look at all the years I lost. What did that get me?* you may wonder. It got me to where I am today. I wouldn't want to do it all over again—it was too much pain—but it helped me to see what it's like to really live.

Today, my life has come full circle. I'm getting married to a partner I've been with for eight years. I have a loving family and a supportive network of so many people. We're a very recovery-oriented family that includes a partner in another twelve-step fellowship, his sons in the program, and an ex-wife who joins us at our table every holiday.

Everybody has a story. This one just happens to be mine, and it's a gift I'm given every single day.

Matthew Read

THE REAL ROMANCE IN LIFE BEGINS WITH FINDING THE COURAGE TO HAVE A HEART-TO-HEART WITH YOURSELF.

Noah benShea

**Don't fight forces;
use them.**

Buckminster Fuller

**Courage is knowing
what not to fear.**

Plato

**Find the courage to let go
of what you can't change.**

Anonymous

We never shall have any more time.

**We have, and we have always had,
all the time there is.**

Arnold Bennett

Only those who will risk going too far

Can possibly find out

How far one can go.

T. S. Eliot

Courage is being scared to death . . .

And saddling up anyway.

John Wayne

**Clear thinking requires courage
rather than intelligence.**

Thomas Szasz

Efforts and courage are not enough

Without purpose and direction.

John F. Kennedy

**Being deeply loved by someone
gives you strength,**

**While loving someone deeply
gives you courage.**

Lao Tzu

Success is not final,

Failure is not fatal:

**It is the courage
to continue that counts.**

Winston S. Churchill

**Courage, above all things,
is the first quality of a warrior.**

Carl von Clausewitz

Fearlessness is not only possible,

It is the ultimate joy.

When you touch non-fear, you are free.

Thich Nhat Hanh

Have courage for the great sorrows in life

And patience for the small ones;

And when you have laboriously
accomplished your daily task,

Go to sleep in peace.

Victor Hugo

It takes courage to grow up

And become who you really are.

E. E. Cummings

Habits are self-encouraging
but not courageous.

Noah benShea

MOST OF US ARE LESS AFRAID OF GOING CRAZY THAN GOING SANE.

Noah benShea

**The most courageous act
is still to think for yourself.**

Aloud.

Coco Chanel

**Above all, be the heroine
of your life, not the victim.**

Nora Ephron

**Courage is the most important
of all the virtues**

Because without courage,

**You can't practice any other
virtue consistently.**

Maya Angelou

**What we stop doing is
sometimes the most
important thing we can do.**

Sophocles

**A ship is safe in harbor,
but that's not what ships are for.**

W. G. T. Shedd

Everyone has talent.

**What's rare is the courage to follow it
to the dark places where it leads.**

Erica Jong

Life shrinks or expands

In proportion to one's courage.

Anaïs Nin

It's a funny thing about life,

**If you refuse to accept
anything but the best,**

You very often get it.

W. Somerset Maugham

Don't be satisfied with stories,

How things have gone with others.

Unfold your own myth.

Rumi

"

COURAGE IS NOT THE ABSENCE OF FEAR BUT HOW WE WRESTLE WITH OUR FEARS.

Noah benShea

All happiness depends on courage and work.

Honoré de Balzac

Courage is found in unlikely places.

J. R. R. Tolkien

Courage isn't having the strength to go on—

It is going on when you don't have strength.

Napoléon Bonaparte

**True strength is keeping
everything together.**

**When everyone expects
you to fall apart.**

Unknown

Courage is grace under pressure.

Ernest Hemingway

**Believe you can and
you're halfway there.**

Theodore Roosevelt

**A man with outward
courage dares to die,**

**A man with inner
courage dares to live.**

Lao Tzu

Freedom lies in being bold.

Robert Frost

**One's dignity may be assaulted,
vandalized, and cruelly mocked,**

**But it can never be taken away
unless it is surrendered.**

Michael J. Fox

"

HONOR YOUR WOUNDS. WOUNDS ARE OPPORTUNITY. HEALING IS STRENGTHENING. SCAR TISSUE IS STRONGER THAN UN-SCARRED SKIN TISSUE.

Noah benShea

Chapter Three

HONESTY

I believe this work gives you the tools to survive on this planet. Helping other people discover the gift of recovery is what keeps me going. I love the magic. Honestly, that's the most rewarding thing there is.

John Southworth

This life of recovery is the only life I know, and it's allowed me to tell someone, "I understand what you're going through," and mean it.

My own experiences have made it possible for me to relate to those I work with and help. I take this work personally. Still, as much as it's a service, it's also an industry that is growing and changing. And I'm encouraged to see the strides we're making.

We've continued to try to educate the public about the realities of addiction and lessen the stigma. And we've seen the Parity Act put into place in recent years, so that insurance companies are compelled to view addiction as a disease and cover treatment accordingly.

Another area where our knowledge is expanding is as it relates to families. We now know that the family is the key. In the past, treatment has included just a few family days, but that's just the beginning. In the same way we monitor the client, we need to monitor the family. Most families are in denial about the help they need, so if they don't get help and address *their issues*, we end up sending someone, still in the early stages of recovery, right back into the lion's den.

We've developed a program for families and we need to hold them accountable, catch them when they're vulnerable. As soon as families see their loved ones in recovery, they think they're ready to come home, but the truth is they're just starting to wake up.

While we've come very far in a relatively short period of time, there's still plenty of progress to be made. It needs to be about more than just "heads in beds." Training matters. And then once people have gone through treatment, we need to do a better job tracking long-term results and better data on the issues at hand.

The US is supposedly leading the way when it comes to treatment, but there's a lot work still to do. At times, it gets overwhelming, but just because you can't do everything doesn't mean you don't do anything. I believe in this process and the benefits it can have for anyone who encounters it.

My life is all about recovery. I live and breathe it. Helping other people discover the gift of recovery is what keeps me going. I love the magic. Honestly, that's the most rewarding thing there is.

John Southworth

ALL PERSONAL TRANSFORMATION REQUIRES HONEST SELF-WITNESSING.

Noah benShea

If you tell the truth

You don't have to remember anything.

Mark Twain

Experience is simply the name we give our mistakes.

Oscar Wilde

You know you're an alcoholic when you misplace things . . . like a decade.

Paul Williams

**I thought I was the
black sheep in the family**

Until I met the rest of the flock.

Anonymous

I never lie because I don't fear anyone.

You only lie when you are afraid.

John Gotti

**Worse than telling a lie is
spending the rest of your life
staying true to a lie.**

Robert Brault

**If you want to ruin the truth,
stretch it.**

Author Unknown

**A fault twice denied
is twice committed.**

French Proverb

**The truth is more important
than the facts.**

Frank Lloyd Wright

Like all valuable commodities, truth is often counterfeited.

James Cardinal Gibbons

Respect for the truth is an acquired taste.

Mark Van Doren

Three things cannot be long hidden: the sun, the moon, the truth.

Buddha

"

ALL SOCIAL DECEIT BEGINS WITH SELF-DECEIT.

Noah benShea

**There are only two mistakes you
can make along the path to the truth:**

**Not going all the way
and not getting started.**

Buddha

**A lie gets halfway around
the world before the truth has
a chance to put its pants on.**

Winston Churchill

**Honesty doesn't always pay,
but dishonesty always costs.**

Michael Josephson

"

NO WELL WITHIN YOU CAN QUENCH YOUR THIRST IF YOUR BUCKET HAS A HOLE IN IT.

Noah benShea

Beware of the half-truth;

**You may have gotten hold
of the wrong half.**

Author Unknown

**Truth is such a rare thing;
"it is delightful to tell it.**

Emily Dickinson

**Honesty pays, but it doesn't seem
to pay enough to suit some people.**

Frank McKinney

**Cherish the friend who tells
you a harsh truth,**

**Wanting ten times more to
tell you a loving lie.**

Robert Brault

**The cruelest lies are
often told in silence.**

Robert Louis Stevenson

**The highest compact we can
make with our fellow is—**

**"Let there be truth between us
two forevermore."**

Ralph Waldo Emerson

**Man is least himself
when he talks in his own person.**

**Give him a mask,
and he will tell you the truth.**

Oscar Wilde

The truth needs so little rehearsal.

Barbara Kingsolver

**There is nothing so powerful as truth,
and often nothing so strange.**

Daniel Webster

"

TRUTH IS BEAUTY, BUT NOT ALL BEAUTY IS ADMIRED.

Noah benShea

**One of the most striking differences
between a cat and a lie**

Is that a cat has only nine lives.

Mark Twain

**Artificial intelligence is when
we think it is wise to tell a lie.**

Noah benShea

Honesty is more than telling others

The dishonesty you tell yourself.

Noah benShea

Chapter Four

EMPOWERMENT

They just needed someone to point them in the right direction. Don't we all? So I continue to show up, rain or shine. I want to be consistent for them in a world that has often proven to be anything but.

Heidi Huerta

Community is huge for me, so when I moved to Nashville and didn't know anybody, I joined a running club. I had no way of knowing it would provide not just the connection I was looking for, but so much more. The club's founder knew I loved volunteering, so he asked if I'd be interested in leading a training program for female residents at a local ministry called The Next Door in preparation for a Heroes in Recovery 6K race.

I hadn't heard of the ministry or the race, but that didn't stop me from recruiting fellow runners and jumping right in. We began coaching these women who had been dealt a rough hand. Many of them were working to rebuild their lives after homelessness, addiction or incarceration—in some cases they were overcoming all three. Initially, I was surprised at how open they were in sharing where they'd been. To hear those stories and see how far these women had already come was inspiring and empowering.

As we trained together for eight weeks leading up to the 6K, there was a shift in me. I came into this thinking of these women as fragile, and in the beginning I was very gentle with them. What I found were strong women, some of whom could outrun me.

That first year, there was one girl, Rachel, who really made an impression on me. In the beginning she said, "I think you're just trying to kill me!" But she stuck with it, and on race day she crossed the finish line. Her two children were there waiting for her, flowers in hand.

Several years later, I'm still so proud of all of them. One finished Nashville's Country Music Marathon less than a year after we trained together. Another went back to school and is studying social work. For some, it's been bumpy, but they're working hard to overcome life's challenges.

I like to think our training helped to empower them, but they were strong long before we met. They always had the drive and determination. They just needed someone to point them in the right direction. Don't we all? So I continue to show up, rain or shine. I want to be consistent for them in a world that has often proven to be anything but.

Today, I work for Heroes in Recovery, the organization that sponsors the 6K race the women and I run together each year.

I'm all about community, relationships and connecting, so my job as community manager is a perfect fit. I love being a resource for people, and now I get to make a living by helping others fulfill their purpose.

As I look forward to my fifth Nashville Heroes 6K with women from The Next Door, I relish my role offering guidance and support. Despite the training, they get apprehensive. *Will I go too slow? Will I have to stop?* But they're learning to pace themselves—in running and in life. Just like me, they're discovering that sometimes you arrive in the place you were meant to be all along just by putting one foot in front of the other.

Heidi Huerta

"

DON'T LET THE PAST KIDNAP YOUR FUTURE.

Noah benShea

The stigma of addiction is wrapped in a shell of shame.

Standing up and speaking up for recovery cracks that shell.

And at Heroes in Recovery our work is to uncover

and recover the best in you.

Rob Waggener, CEO FRN

As we look ahead into the next century,

Leaders will be those who empower others.

Bill Gates

For me, it's never been about fitness.

It's always been about helping to empower people.

Jillian Michaels

**The curious paradox is that when
I accept myself just as I am,
then I can change.**

Carl Rogers

**When you say yes to others
do not say no to yourself.**

Unknown

**It is never too late to be
what you might have been.**

George Eliot

**Ultimately, the only power to
which man should aspire is that which
he exercises over himself.**

Elie Weisel

**Do the thing and you will
have the power.**

Ralph Waldo Emerson

Some day is no day.

Anonymous

**What you could do tomorrow
should be begun tonight.**

Scottish Proverb

**Power is not revealed by
striking hard or often,
but by striking true.**

Honoré de Balzac

**The most common way
people give up their power is
by thinking they don't have any.**

Alice Walker

Being powerful is like being a lady.

**If you have to tell people
you are, you aren't.**

Margaret Thatcher

**Most powerful is he who
has himself in his own power.**

Seneca

**We must leave our
mark on our life**

**While we have it
in our power.**

Isak Dinesen

Mastering others is strength,

Mastering yourself is true power.

Lao Tzu

You must be the change

You want to see in the world.

Mahatma Gandhi

He who gains a victory
over other men is strong,

But he who gains a victory
over himself is all-powerful.

Lao Tzu

POWER IS OFTEN NO MORE COMPLICATED THAN EXERCISING YOUR POWER OVER YOUR FEARS.

Noah benShea

I am not what I ought to be,

I am not what I want to be,

I am not what I hope to be in another world,

But still I am not what I once used to be, and
by the grace of God I am what I am.

John Newton

Great works are performed not by
strength but by perseverance.

Samuel Johnson

It is better to conquer yourself,

Than to win a thousand battles.

Then the victory is yours.

It cannot be taken from you,

Not by angels or by demons, heaven or hell.

Buddha

"

THE POWER TO BE WHO YOU MIGHT YET BECOME IS VERY BECOMING.

Noah benShea

**Forgiveness is the
final form of love.**

Reinhold Niebuhr

Determination is power.

Charles Simmons

**Circumstances are beyond
human control,
but our conduct is in our own power.**

Benjamin Disraeli

"

THERE IS A POWER IN PUTTING YOURSELF DOWN, AND HOLDING YOURSELF DOWN, AND HAVING THE POWER NOT TO.

Noah benShea

**I am still determined to be cheerful and
happy, in whatever situation I may be,**

**For I have also learned from experience that
the greater part of our happiness or misery**

**Depends upon our dispositions,
and not upon our circumstances.**

Martha Washington

Your have two great powers.

The power to say, "Yes."

And the power to say, "No."

**And the greater power is
knowing when to say what.**

Noah benShea

**Most powerful is he who
has himself in his own power.**

Lucius Annaeus Seneca

"

THE POWER OF THOUGHT IS A POWER WE OFTEN DON'T GIVE A THOUGHT.

Noah benShea

**Like all weak men he laid
an exaggerated stress
on not changing one's mind.**

W. Somerset Maugham

**The price of greatness
is responsibility.**

Winston Churchill

**Do not pray for tasks
equal to your powers.**

**Pray for powers equal
to your tasks.**

Phillips Brooks

" YOU ARE THE KING OF YOU. WEAR THE CROWN WITH RESPONSIBILITY. TO YOU.

Noah benShea

**What lies in our power to do,
it lies in our power not to do.**

Aristotle

**Of all the things you
can make in life**

**Remember the difference
you make in your life.**

Noah benShea

Chapter Five

RENEWAL

What gets me out of bed every morning is hope.

Judith Landau

As a South African, I grew up essentially in a war zone under apartheid, and my own family was heavily involved. My father's mission was to equalize the infant mortality rate in Africa with that of first world countries. There was a sense of mission and purpose. Today, my hope still comes from a sense of purpose, and the knowledge that we all have an inherent resiliency that gives us the ability to recover.

I'm an expert in trauma, which may seem like a heavy line of work, but despite the weightiness attached to the word, I see trauma as an opportunity for growth. We are all faced with trauma more frequently than we think. It doesn't just come from extreme situations like death, war, or violent crime. A family dealing with three or more transitions at a time is going to be thrown off-track.

Even good transitions like a sought after new job or the birth of a child can throw us off balance. And when we go through trauma, we lose our resources. We tend to keep going rather than stopping to deal with what's going on.

Addiction slows us down and forces us to pay attention. I see addiction as resilience in action. When an individual or a family is severely traumatized, when there's major trauma at any level, what happens is that people are overcome by grief and loss. Addiction draws everyone's attention and they have to deal with that instead of their own grief.

I help the addicted to access their capacity to remain connected to those they love, their neighborhoods, and their communities, coming out on the other side stronger than they were before.

When you look at risk-taking like addiction, the more connected we are, the less risks we're compelled to take. That's why all of our interventions are based on accessing that inherent resiliency and stopping the process.

My approach, growing up in community, is to bring the whole community in to teach you and look for where the resources and resiliency are. Don't demonize the community. Teach the therapists to involve the family. They need help, too.

What gets me out of bed every morning is hope and having a sense of mission. I love to wake up and see the beauty around me and know that however bad things are, they can be changed. It's worth working toward.

Judith Landau

"

NOBODY EVER BECAME A BETTER ANYTHING WHO WASN'T WORKING ON BEING A BETTER PERSON.

Noah benShea

The chains of habit are generally too small to be felt until they are too strong to be broken.

Samuel Johnson

The human capacity for survival and renewal is awesome.

Isabel Allende

Renewal is not something we need to pursue though it often requires us to slow down

To achieve renewal's pursuit of us.

Noah benShea

"

SOBRIETY IS A GIFT. PRAYER IS A THANK YOU NOTE.

Noah benShea

**Habit, if not resisted,
soon becomes necessity.**

St. Augustine

**It's never too late
to start over.**

Anonymous

What is the scent of water?

**Renewal. The goodness of God
coming down like dew.**

Elizabeth Goudge

"

DENIAL IS DEFEAT IN THE MAKING.

Noah benShea

Often the greatest personal power

**Is not what you grab but
what you can release.**

Noah benShea

**There are no miracles for
those that have no faith in them.**

French Proverb

We don't even know how strong we are

Until we are forced to bring

That hidden strength forward.

Isabel Allende

Renewal is not something to achieve.

It is something to witness.

All the world is in renewal.

Including you.

Not to know this doesn't change a thing.

Renewal is a fact of life.

Face the facts.

Noah benShea

As part of our renewal—

We need to fight problems,

Not just wait for them to take place.

Nong Duc Manh

"

THERE IS NOTHING WRONG IN YOU THAT CAN'T BE CURED BY WHAT IS RIGHT IN YOU. ALL HEALING INVOLVES SELF-HEALING.

Noah benShea

Miracles are not contrary to nature,

**But only contrary to what
we know about nature.**

Saint Augustine

**The pursuit of perfection is wrong
before it is right.**

**Perfection is shadowed
by tension and routinely confuses
anxiety with achievement.**

Noah benShea

**There is no sadder sight
than a young pessimist.**

Mark Twain

"

WHAT WE THINK SHOULD HAPPEN IS OFTEN JUST THAT.

Noah benShea

**Concern should drive us into
action and not into a depression.**

Karen Horney

**The greatest evil that can befall man is that
he should come to think ill of himself.**

Johann Wolfgang von Goethe

**Every stop on our journey
was once a destination.**

Even destiny is a whistle stop.

Noah benShea

As wave is driven by wave

And each, pursued, pursues
the wave ahead . . .

What was before is left behind,

What never was is now,

And every passing moment is renewed.

Ovid

Only from the alliance of the one,

Working with and through the other,

Are great things born.

Antoine de Saint-Exupery

We've all been in the lost and found.

Lose the least in you; claim the best.

Noah benShea

"

A NEW TOMORROW IS THE ONLY TOMORROW THERE IS.

Noah benShea

**It is not because things are
difficult that we do not dare,**

**It is because we do not dare
that they are difficult.**

Seneca

**No saint without a past;
no sinner without a future.**

St. Augustine

**Possibility and problems
are often home grown.**

**Pay attention to what
you are watering.**

Noah benShea

"

THE BEST WAY TO TAKE OUT A THORN IS WITH ANOTHER THORN. THE BEST WAY TO GET RID OF A BAD HABIT IS WITH A GOOD HABIT.

Noah benShea

**It is a narrow mind,
which cannot look at a subject
from various points of view.**

George Eliot

When this ultimate crisis comes . . .

When there is no way out—

**That is the very moment when
we explode from within**

And the totally other emerges:

The sudden surfacing of a strength,

A security of unknown origin,

**Welling up from beyond reason,
rational expectation, and hope.**

Émile Durkheim

**All the wonders you seek
are within yourself.**

Sir Thomas Brown

"

THE ULTIMATE MOMENT IN ANY EVENT IS WHEN WE REALIZE THERE IS NO ULTIMATE MOMENT. ONLY MOMENTS.

Noah benShea

"

"

THOSE WHO SAY THEY ARE ONLY "KILLING A LITTLE TIME" ARE LITTERING IN THE WORST WAY. THEY ARE LITTERING THEIR MOMENTS.

Noah benShea

Wisdom is knowing what to do next.

Virtue is doing it.

David Star Jordan

**Progress never marches
in a parade.**

Walter Winchell

The old go to sleep with memories.

The young go to sleep with dreams.

**But neither memories nor dreams
sleep through the night.**

Noah benShea

Chapter Six

HOPE

One day, I was reading The Thinking Person's Guide to Sobriety. I had a joint burning in the ashtray and a glass of Crown Royal at my side. That's when she walked by and asked, "Aren't you supposed to be sober when you read that?"

Darren Kavinoky

To have hope; you have to first have honesty. So, here goes. To be truthful, my addiction started when I was thirteen. I was a fat kid and uncomfortable in my own skin. I somehow ended up at a party with all the cool kids. I had no business being there, of course, so when a cool kid passed me a joint, I took it. I felt like I'd been offered an opportunity to be in the club. It all changed in that moment. I no longer felt the unbearable weight of being me. And I wanted to feel this way every day.

I flunked out of college because I stopped attending class. I was too busy getting loaded. Convinced that my location was the problem, my family brought me to Los Angeles. Not surprisingly, my problems followed. After my fifth arrest—here's a surprise—I talked my way into law school. But I also got a job for a lawyer who drank just like me. I attended class at night, went to law school basically in a blackout, and my grades reflected it.

Still, somehow, I managed to graduate and pass the bar exam. Then I went to work for a firm that did what I felt was really boring stuff. At the end of the day, I'd clock out and go over to the criminal court, where the action was. I dreamed of doing that some day, and when the opportunity came along, I grabbed it with both hands.

Initially, I became a criminal defense lawyer because I thought it would bring a lot of excitement to my life, and I'd get to hang out with a better class of drug dealer. It was right around the time of the O. J. Simpson trial, a very hot time to be a lawyer. I became very successful, but I was also busy battling my own demons. My addictions to Xanax, cocaine, and alcohol took their toll on my career. I kept hitting bottom and then I'd find a new bottom. My wife threw me out and my dog left me; my life had become a bad country song. I ended up homeless, working at a store moving furniture. I had no clients as an attorney. I'd been to rehab five times and failed every time.

Then one day, I was sitting in the study at my estranged wife's house reading *The Thinking Person's Guide to Sobriety*. I had a joint burning in the ashtray and a glass of Crown Royal at my side. That's when she walked by and asked, "Aren't you supposed to be sober when you read that?" It was a moment of clarity. That was May 9, 2000.

My wife and I eventually reconciled and just celebrated twenty years of marriage. Together, we have a thirteen-year-old daughter who's never seen Daddy loaded. My career has undergone an overhaul as well. I got into this line of work for one reason, and I've stayed in it for a completely different one. It's no longer about getting close to criminals. Through my law firm and 1-800-N-O-C-U-F-F-S (662-8337), I'm offering assistance to a population that's very underserved. I get to help people.

My specialization in this area has led to work on TV, as a legal analyst for shows like *The Insider*, news networks including CNN, as well as hosting *Deadly Sins* and other shows for Investigation Discovery Network.

In my daily work, I'm steeped in this behavior, so it's important to take time to share my experience in an inspirational way. Everyone is either an example of what's possible or a warning of a what's possible. And it's never too late. As long as you're drawing breath, there's the possibility of amazing transformation. Have hope!

Darren Kavinoky

"

IF PEOPLE DO NOT GROW INTO WHO THEY MIGHT YET BECOME THEY GROW INTO WHO THEY WERE.

Noah benShea

Hope is being able to see that there is light despite all of the darkness.

Desmond Tutu

Hope is the last thing ever lost.

Italian Proverb

What is Hope?

A star that gleaming O'er the future's troubled sky,

Struggles, tremulously beaming,

To reveal what there may lie.

R. A. P.

**Everything that is done in the world
is done by hope.**

Martin Luther

Believe in your self,

And believe in more than your self.

Noah benShea

**What lies behind us,
and what lies before us,**

**Are small matters compared
to what lies within us.**

Ralph Waldo Emerson

"

GOING THROUGH CHANGE IS NEVER SMALL CHANGE.

Noah benShea

**Regrets are the natural property
of gray hairs.**

Charles Dickens

**All men dream:
but not equally.**

T. E. Lawrence

Hold fast to dreams,

For if dreams die

Life is a broken-winged bird,

That cannot fly.

Langston Hughes

"

IF YOU HOPE TO BECOME BETTER, PUT YOUR HOPE TO WORK.

Noah benShea

**Ideals are like stars;
you cannot touch them with hands.**

Carl Shurz

No dark; no stars.

Noah benShea

**All human wisdom is
contained in these two words,
"Wait and Hope."**

Alexandre Dumas

"

YOU ONLY HAVE TWO ARMS, IF YOU'RE HUGGING THE PAST YOU WON'T BE ABLE TO EMBRACE THE FUTURE.

Noah benShea

**They say a person needs just three things
to be truly happy in this world:
someone to love, something to do,
and something to hope for.**

Tom Bodett

**And now these three remain:
faith, hope and love.**

But the greatest of these is love.

Corinthians 13:13

**Life is what happens while you're
making other plans.**

Unknown

**If what you want isn't happening,
be the happening.**

Noah benShea

Don't be afraid to go out on a limb.

That's where the fruit is.

Unknown

**Believe that life is worth living and your
belief will help create the fact.**

William James

"

IF YOU FEEL YOU ARE LESS THAN YOU HOPED TO BE, DON'T ABANDON HOPE, AND YOU WILL NOT BE ABANDONED.

Noah benShea

**This is where you begin,
beginning right now.**

Noah benShea

**Do not dwell in the past,
do not dream of the future**

**Concentrate the mind
on the present moment.**

Buddha

**Be faithful in small things
because it is in them that
your strength lies.**

Anonymous

"

THE MEASURE OF SUCCESS BEGINS WITH TAKING MEASURED STEPS. AND KNOWING HOPE IS BEYOND MEASURE.

Noah benShea

What we wish, we readily believe,

**And what we ourselves think,
we imagine others think also.**

Julius Caesar

**It's the possibility that keeps me going,
not the guarantee.**

Nicholas Sparks

**There is nothing like a dream
to create the future.**

Victor Hugo

Don't confuse falling with failing.

We all fall.

We all fail.

Because we are all frail.

This is the brotherhood and sisterhood we all share.

And is the shared heroism of day-to-day living.

Noah benShea

What would life be if we had no courage to attempt anything?

Vincent van Gogh

There is a secret medicine given only to those who hurt so hard they can't hope.

Rumi

"

HOPE'S MAGIC IS HOPE.

Noah benShea

Everything that is done in this world is done by hope.

Martin Luther

Hope is self-conceiving.

Hope is born from hope.

Noah benShea

Hell is hopelessness.

It is no accident that above the entrance to Dante's hell is the inscription:

Leave behind all hope, you who enter here.

Fyodor Dostoevsky

"

NO MATTER HOW DARK THE ROOM YOU LIVE IN, HOPE IS A WINDOW; OPEN YOURS.

Noah benShea

**Where there is no hope,
it is incumbent on us to invent it.**

Albert Camus

**Hope is your right and
your responsibility.**

Hope to know both.

Noah benShea

**Sadness is but a wall
between two gardens.**

Kahlil Gibran

"

HOPE IS NEVER LOST. IT IS US WHO LOSE OUR WAY TO HOPE.

Noah benShea

**Hope's only disappointment
is when we are not hopeful.**

Noah benShea

Hope sees with eyes shut.

And sleeps only to dream.

Noah benShea

**We are people with lanterns
going in search of a light.**

Noah benShea

"

YOU'RE NOT LOST IN A DREAM; YOU ARE ONLY DREAMING YOU ARE LOST.

Noah benShea

**If winter comes,
can spring be far behind?**

Percy Bysshe Shelley

**When despair is employed,
hope's work is hope.**

Noah benShea

**Rock bottom became
the solid foundation on which
I rebuilt my life.**

J. K. Rowling

"

HOPE IS EVERY ARTIST'S BRUSH. PICK UP YOUR BRUSH. YOUR CANVAS IS WAITING TO SEE WHO YOU WILL BE.

Noah benShea

**In your life you are the painter,
the paint, and the painting.**

Noah benShea

**The only way we'll get
freedom for ourselves is to identify
ourselves with every oppressed
people in the world.**

Malcolm X

Hope and fear are both addictions.

Freedom is choosing your addiction.

Noah benShea

"

HOPE HAS NO COST BUT THE COST OF HAVING NO HOPE.

Noah benShea

"

HOPE SHOULD BE THE FIRST THING YOU PACK IN YOUR HOPE CHEST.

Noah benShea

"

Hope is a breathing lesson.

Inhale hope.

Exhale hope.

And again.

And again.

**Without hope life is
a self-strangulation.**

Noah benShea

**Built into every stumbling
block is a building block.**

Noah benShea

Carry the fire.

Cormac McCarthy

**If you want a guarantee in life,
buy a vacuum cleaner.**

Noah benShea

**Yes, hope is hard work,
but it is the best work
we can hope for.**

Noah benShea

**Hope always has
a help-wanted sign.**

Noah benShea

Chapter Seven

FORGIVENESS

When those in need feel the healing force, they begin to understand that the opportunity to heal is real. Then I am really happy—I truly am.

Brian O'Shea

Some of us come to this line of work through education, others through experience. My first childhood memories are of almost being beaten to death by my father, who suffered mental illness and substance use disorder. That gave me a unique point of view going forward and informs the work I do today as an interventionist. It also made forgiveness a difficult concept for me for quite a while.

Along my own journey, I learned to forgive others, but those early experiences remained beyond the grasp of grace. Then I reached a point where I needed forgiveness from a couple of people I couldn't find. I was at a crossroads: If I accepted the idea that

I had this disease and some behavioral health disorders, and I needed to allow myself to be forgiven, then I had to see that my father struggled with those same things and needed forgiveness, too.

It all starts with forgiveness. So many people can't move into recovery and a successful life because they can't find the way to self-forgiveness and self-compassion. We need forgiveness in order to believe that we deserve recovery and to heal. Forgiving yourself becomes crucial to the process; if you can't, you'll never be able to help others.

My recovery life started when I was ten years old as an "Ala-tot" in family programs. For me, it was about finding hope. It's been a long journey, and it's one I'm still on. Hope for me looks like being able to live my life free from trauma, free from anger, free from hate. It's about a deeper capacity to love and be loved, something I'm so grateful to be able to help others find as well.

Addiction is baffling. It defies logic. It's incredibly painful when someone you love is lying to you. These behaviors are so irrational. Eventually it brings us to a point of hopelessness. But fortunately there are people who can help restore hope to these situations.

Being able to offer that hope to someone else is what keeps me going. Helping an individual move out of active addiction and into recovery refills and recharges me. A bigger piece that fuels my passion for this work is removing fear from an entire family system and reconnecting them with the ideas of resilience, hope, and a sense of victory for the future.

The gift of my years is that I've been through a lot and seen much. The result of that is you can't intimidate me. Fame, wealth, power, they don't intimidate or impress me. I'm also 100 percent certain that someone's wealth, power, and fame won't protect them.

When you or someone you love is ferociously mentally ill, it's very frightening. And people often have no idea how to respond to it or deal with it. Many, sadly, hold themselves back from happiness, afraid to take that leap of faith that there's a different way to live.

Each person's story is different. Behavioral health challenges, mental health challenges, addiction, etc.—they're all the same, but how each person experiences them is different. And we all need to have the opportunity to tell our story.

By listening, really listening, we can establish credibility and earn the right to speak some truth into the situation. Then as healers, we can come in with a mixture of well-sculpted advice, transparency, and joy.

When those in need feel the healing force, they begin to understand that the opportunity to heal is real. And then, then I am really happy—I truly am.

Brian O'Shea

IN ORDER TO BOUNCE BACK YOU HAVE TO ADMIT YOU'RE FALLING.

Noah benShea

The weak can never forgive.

**Forgiveness is the attribute
of the strong.**

Mahatma Gandhi

**To be a Christian means to
forgive the inexcusable**

**Because God has forgiven the
inexcusable in you.**

C. S. Lewis

It is surely better to pardon too much,

Than to condemn too much.

George Eliot

**I have always found that
mercy bears richer fruits**

than strict justice.

Abraham Lincoln

**Gold cannot be pure,
and people cannot be perfect.**

Chinese Proverb

**How few there are who have courage
enough to own their faults,**

Or resolution enough to mend them.

Benjamin Franklin

**A happy marriage is the union
of two good forgivers.**

Robert Quillen

**To forgive means pardoning
the unpardonable.**

G. K. Chesterton

**Resentment is like drinking
poison and then hoping
it will kill your enemies.**

Nelson Mandela

**Not forgiving is like drinking
rat poison and then waiting
for the rat to die.**

Anne Lamott

**The ability to forgive others
is premised on our ability
to forgive ourselves.**

Noah benShea

**To err is human,
to forgive, divine.**

Alexander Pope

"

SELF-FORGIVENESS REQUIRES SELF-ACCOUNTABILITY NOT SELF-ABUSE.

Noah benShea

IF YOU DO NOT FEEL WORTHY OF LOVE, ALL THE MORE YOUR NEED TO BE LOVED.

Noah benShea

**It's not the perfect who need love;
it is the imperfect.**

Oscar Wilde

**Forgiveness is the fragrance
that the violet sheds on the
heel that has crushed it.**

Mark Twain

**One of the keys to happiness
is a bad memory.**

Rita Mae Brown

**To be wronged is nothing,
unless you continue to remember it.**

Confucius

Forgive, forget, and move on.

Anonymous

**Resentment, born of weakness,
harms no one more than
the weak person himself.**

Friedrich Nietzsche

"

FORGIVE THOSE WHO HAVE NOT ASKED TO BE FORGIVEN. AND FORGIVE YOURSELF FOR YOUR DELAY IN FORGIVING.

Noah benShea

"

FORGIVING IS CROSS ELEVATING. FORGIVING LIFTS BOTH THE GIVER AND THE RECEIVER.

Noah benShea

**Reputation is what others think of us;
character is what God knows of us.**

Shannon L. Alder

**Self-forgiveness is nothing more
or less than self-love.**

Noah benShea

**Forgiveness is
the final form of love.**

Reinhold Niebuhr

**To the degree you insist
that you must suffer,**

**You insist on the suffering
of others as well.**

Stephen Levine

Life is an adventure in forgiveness

Norman Cousins

**When we don't forgive our faults
we lose access to our virtues.**

Noah benShea

"

IF YOU'RE WONDERING WHAT YOU CAN GIVE YOURSELF TRY SELF- FORGIVENESS.

Noah benShea

**You will never forgive anyone
more than God has
already forgiven you.**

Max Lucado

**When I let go of what I am,
I become what I might be.**

**When I let go of what I have,
I receive what I need.**

Lao Tzu

**Man is free at the moment
he wishes to be.**

Voltaire

Forgive yourself when you least deserve it for that is when you need it most.

Forgive others when they least deserve it for that is when you are most forgiven.

Noah benShea

There is nothing noble about suffering except the love and forgiveness with which we meet it.

Stephen Levine

Compassion literally means
to care passionately.

To be self-compassionate means to care
passionately about who we are.

The opposite of love is not hate.

The opposite of love is indifference.

The opposite of being
self-compassionate is to be
indifferent to who we are.

Compassion is God's grace.

Self-compassion gives us
access to God's grace.

Self-compassion is
the grace we offer ourselves.

Absent of grace we are
absent of peace.

Noah benShea

Chapter Eight

FAITH

To have faith requires us to be of faith.
Faith is a verb. Recovery is an action word.
Recovery requires us to take action in our
lives. And have faith. Put your faith and
not your fears in charge.

Noah benShea

It has long seemed to me that anyone who might know they are a healer is someone who knows that all of us—at some point—need healing. And while cures are many, the portal to any cure is faith.

While many people assume that faith is an issue solely between us and God, or our God, or a great cosmic truth, too often we elevate the issue of faith into irrelevance.

God is *all*, so having faith is something between us and *all*. That means we need to have faith in our wife, our children, our friends, and our ability to have faith in others requires us to have faith in ourselves.

So, anyone in hope of recovery needs to begin that journey by discovering or rediscovering faith.

This is not an issue of Sunday pew faith but seven-day-a-week, day-to-day, moment-to-moment, rest of your life, 24/7/365 faith.

Healers are not people who have achieved faith and can move on. Any of us can, at any moment, find our balance and lose our balance.

Who among us hasn't discovered that in this brief life we can be in the dark at high noon, and we can be guided by the brightest stars on the darkest night of our lives. No one has ever found his or her way who has not felt lost, but do not confuse feeling lost with being lost.

To have faith requires us to be of faith. Faith is a verb, and recovery is an action word. Recovery requires us to take action in our lives. And have faith. Put your faith and not your fears in charge.

Noah benShea

66

GOD IS NEVER SO WITH YOU AS WHEN YOU FEEL ALONE.

Noah benShea

Prayer is a path

Where there is none.

Noah benShea

The wind in your face
may be God

Blowing you kisses.

Noah benShea

All the world is made of faith,
and trust, and pixie dust.

J. M. Barrie

"

GOD MAKES HOUSE CALLS, BUT YOU'VE GOT TO MAKE THE CALL.

Noah benShea

" FAITH SEES AROUND THE CORNER TAKE A PEEK!

Noah benShea

**Faithless is he that says
farewell when the road darkens.**

J. R. R. Tolkien

**God will not look you over
for medals, degrees, or diplomas
but for scars.**

Elbert Hubbard

**Never be afraid to trust an
unknown future to a known God.**

Corrie ten Boom

The function of prayer is not to influence God, but rather to change the nature of the one who prays.

Søren Kierkegaard

An army of sheep led by a lion will defeat an army of lions led by a sheep.

Persian Proverb

Do not be afraid,

Our fate cannot be taken from us; it is a gift.

Dante Alighieri

"

PUT YOUR FAITH AND NOT YOUR FEARS IN CHARGE.

Noah benShea

**However mean your life is,
meet it and live it;**

**Do not shun it and
call it hard names . . .**

**The fault-finder will find faults,
even in paradise.**

Henry David Thoreau

**Follow your bliss and
the universe will open doors for you**

Where there were only walls.

Joseph Campbell

**It's hard to beat someone
who never gives up.**

Babe Ruth

"

WE ARE NOT DEFINED BY THE TIMES WE LIVE IN BUT BY WHO WE ARE IN THE TIME WE ARE GIVEN.

Noah benShea

" FAITH IS A VERB. ACTION WORDS REQUIRE ACTION.

Noah benShea

If you pray to grow or grow anything in life you have to plant hope to reap faith.

Noah benShea

God is family to people of faith.

Noah benShea

In gratitude find prayer.

In prayer find faith.

In faith find grace.

In grace find peace.

In peace find gratitude.

Noah benShea

"

EVERY FIRST STEP IS A LEAP OF FAITH.

Noah benShea

**Faith is not so much
something we believe;
faith is something we live.**

Joseph B. Wirthlin

Don't have faith—be of faith.

Noah benShea

**Some things have to be
believed to be seen.**

Madeleine L'Engle

**All our reasoning ends
in surrender to feeling.**

Blaise Pascal

**Trust the instinct to the end,
though you can render no reason.**

Ralph Waldo Emerson

**Believe there is a great
power silently working
all things for good,**

**Behave yourself and
never mind the rest.**

Beatrix Potter

**Faith is not something to grasp,
it is a state to grow into.**

Mahatma Gandhi

**Faith consists in believing
what reason cannot.**

Voltaire

**Because you believed I was
capable of behaving decently,
I did.**

Paulo Coelho

**Sometimes when you
lose your way,
you find YOURSELF.**

Mandy Hale

**You can't know,
you can only believe—or not.**

C. S. Lewis

**Faith is the bird that
feels the light and sings
when the dawn is still dark.**

Rabindranath Tagore

**To believe a thing impossible
is to make it so.**

French Proverb

**Faith does not
eliminate questions.**

**But faith knows
where to take them.**

Elisabeth Elliot

**Indecision becomes
decision with time.**

Anonymous

**God helps those
who help themselves.**

Algernon Sidney

**There lives more faith
in honest doubt, believe me,
than in half the creeds.**

Alfred Lord Tennyson

**We are ever striving after
what is forbidden, and coveting
what is denied us.**

Ovid

**Even the merest gesture is holy
if it is filled with faith.**

Franz Kafka

**There are some places in life
where you can only go alone.**

**Embrace the beauty
of your solo journey.**

Mandy Hale

**Commit to the Lord whatever you do,
and he will establish your plans.**

Proverbs 16:3

Just because you can explain it doesn't mean it's not still a miracle.

Terry Pratchett

Faith is not the clinging to a shrine but an endless pilgrimage of the heart.

Abraham Joshua Heschel

God may be a small still voice,

And the Devil may run a lot of loud ads,

So know when to adjust the volume in your life.

Noah benShea

**The art of medicine consists
in amusing the patient while
nature cures the disease.**

Voltaire

**Real religion is the transformation
of anxiety into laughter.**

Alan W. Watts

**Faith is not only seeing things unseen;
it is also seeing in ways
you have not seen.**

Noah benShea

" TO HEAR THE TRUTH, LISTEN FOR YOUR DEAFNESS.

Noah benShea

**Faith is knowledge within the heart,
beyond the reach of proof.**

Kahlil Gibran

Have faith have faith.

**When you have nothing else
have faith.**

Francine Rivers

Take the first step in faith.

**You don't have to see the whole,
just take the first step.**

Dr. Martin Luther King Jr.

"

TO UNCOVER YOUR FAITH, STOP BURYING IT. THE OBVIOUS IS OFTEN HIDDEN IN ITS OBVIOUSNESS.

Noah benShea

**It's never too late to be
who you might have been.**

T. S. Elliot

**What will work for us in life
usually requires us**

Working on what doesn't work for us.

**If this sounds trite,
remember the truth can be trite**

And no less true.

Noah benShea

Addiction is faith in failure.

**Addiction offers a man dying of thirst
directions to a mirage.**

Noah benShea

**Things don't have to be good
for you to be great.**

Noah benShea

Prayer gets you high.

Noah benShea

**Even superstars are
stars in the dark.**

Noah benShea

"

DO NOT CONFUSE FEELING LOST WITH BEING LOST.

Noah benShea

Chapter Nine

INSPIRATION

You need someone to point the way,

Someone who has the directions and can show you

How to get where you want to go.

Now, I can do that for others.

It's a role I was called to through pain and experience.

And I relish my role in life.

Tondra Frisby

Getting clean wasn't initially my idea. It all started when I received a nudge from a judge. After winding up in court, I was graciously offered treatment in lieu of conviction, so I agreed to get help for my problem with crack cocaine.

I was exposed to addiction at an early age. Growing up, I felt caught between two different worlds. My parents divorced when

I was nine. My dad had been abusive to my mom and brother but not to me, so I was resented in my house after he left. I always felt alone. As a result, I was always very wary of doing anything that might draw positive attention or earn me any praise. I was working very hard behind the scenes to not create any additional resentment, and it was a lot of responsibility for a teen girl.

On weekend visits, I tagged along with my dad to the bars where I'd hang out shooting pool. "You're Bronco's daughter," they'd say. That became my identity. He was an alcoholic, and by junior high, I was well on my way to developing a drinking problem of my own. From there I moved on to selling drugs.

Fast-forward twenty years and I had two boys of my own. My disease was so cunning that each time I got pregnant I quit all drinking, drugs, and cigarettes for nine months. That helped me think I didn't have a problem because I was able to stop. My mom ended up raising my boys for almost six years. Then came that offer from the judge.

I resigned from being the CEO of my life in 1996. God is my CEO. He knows where I'm supposed to go, and I trust him to get me there. It's such a relief not to drive. Now I'm buckled into that passenger seat and just enjoying the ride.

In recovery, I worked as a food and beverage manager for an indoor water park resort, but by 2007 I really started feeling like there was something more I needed to be doing. I started watching the TV show *Intervention* on A&E. It was hard to see the beginning of each episode, but I was attracted to the part where that person comes in and gives that gift to a family, the opportunity to get treatment. I wanted to do that.

I became a certified interventionist, the only one in the state of Ohio, and I love what I get to do. I run my own intervention service, which I started in 2007. I focus on young people—adolescents or young adults eighteen to thirty-five years old—maybe because I see a little of myself in them.

I spent almost twenty years in active addition and nineteen years in recovery, so I've known both sides. Today, I use my past to build an alliance with my clients and show them that someone knows who you are and why you keep doing what you're doing. Their family may not get it, but I've been there. I use a lot of analogies because that's how it had to make sense to me. Say you're driving down the road, and you know where you want to go, and it's a great place, but you don't have GPS. You get off on the wrong exit. You have no way to recalculate. You need someone to point the way, someone who has the directions and can show you how to get where you want to go. Now, I can do that for others. It's a role I was called to through pain and experience. And I relish my role in life.

Tondra Frisby

"

DISCOVER WHAT YOUR LIFE MIGHT YET BE WHEN YOU TURN YOUR STUMBLING BLOCKS INTO BUILDING BLOCKS.

Noah benShea

**We know that pain is part of life;
suffering is optional.**

Living is about exercising your options.

Good living is about exercising daily.

Lee Pepper, Chief Marketing Officer FRN

**Your problem is how
are you going to spend**

**This one odd and precious life
you have been issued.**

Anne Lamott

What you do makes a difference,

**And you have to decide what kind of
difference you want to make.**

Jane Goodall

**The flower that blooms
in adversity is the rarest and
most beautiful of all.**

Mulan

**If you stay on the excuse train
you'll miss your train.**

Noah benShea

**The person who says
it cannot be done**

**Should not interrupt the person
who is doing it.**

Chinese Proverb

"

HEAVEN WEEPS FOR THOSE WHO CAN'T CRY BUT NOT FOR THOSE WHO DON'T TRY.

Noah benShea

**There are no traffic jams
along the extra mile.**

Roger Staubach

**If we did the things
we are capable of,
we would astound ourselves.**

Thomas Edison

**When everything seems
to be going against you,**

**remember that the airplane takes off
against the wind, not with it.**

Henry Ford

**The most common way
people give up their power is
by thinking they don't have any.**

Alice Walker

**Observe due measure,
for right timing is in all things
the most important factor.**

Hesiod

Nothing is impossible;

**The word itself says,
"I'm possible!"**

Audrey Hepburn

THE HERE AND NOW IS NOW AND HERE.

Noah benShea

**Whether you think you can
or you think you can't,
you're right.**

Henry Ford

**You are the first person
who can help you.**

**And you are the first person
who can stop you.**

Noah benShea

**Remember that not getting
what you want is sometimes
a wonderful stroke of luck.**

The Dalai Lama

"

A LOT OF US GET DRAGGED KICKING AND SCREAMING TO A BETTER PLACE.

Noah benShea

**Do not spoil what you have
by desiring what you have not;**

**Remember that what you now have
was once among the things
you only hoped for.**

Epicurus

**Everything you've ever wanted
is on the other side of fear.**

George Addair

**I can't change the direction of the wind,
but I can adjust my sails
to always reach my destination.**

Jimmy Dean

**How wonderful it is that
nobody need wait a single moment
before starting to improve the world.**

Anne Frank

**If the wind will not serve,
take to the oars.**

Latin Proverb

Start where you are.

Use what you have.

Do what you can.

Arthur Ashe

"

DESTINY IS INFLUENCED BY DECISION.

Noah benShea

"

THE AVERAGE CHILD WILL FALL 300 TIMES BEFORE THEY LEARN TO WALK.

Noah benShea

**Believe you can and
you're halfway there.**

Theodore Roosevelt

For too many of us,

A will is something we leave behind

**Rather than something
we exercise while we're here.**

Noah benShea

Be willing to find the will.

And you will.

Noah benShea

"

WHAT WE WILL ONE DAY DO IS ALWAYS A DAY AWAY.

Noah benShea

"

**If you hear a voice within you say,
"You cannot paint,"**

Then by all means paint

And that voice will be silenced.

Vincent Van Gogh

**There is only one way
to avoid criticism:
Do nothing, say nothing,
and be nothing.**

Aristotle

Ask and it will be given to you;

Search, and you will find;

**Knock and the door will
be opened for you.**

Jesus Christ

**Too many of us are
not living our dreams
because we are living our fears.**

Les Brown

I didn't fail the test.

**I just found 100 ways
to do it wrong.**

Benjamin Franklin

**The power of imagination
makes us infinite.**

John Muir

**We can easily forgive a child
who is afraid of the dark,**

**The real tragedy of life is when
men are afraid of the light.**

Plato

Nothing will work unless you do.

Maya Angelou

**What we achieve inwardly
will change outer reality.**

Plutarch

**You must do the things
you think you cannot do.**

Eleanor Roosevelt

**Start by doing what is necessary,
then do what is possible, and suddenly
you are doing the impossible.**

St. Francis of Assisi

**Do or do not.
There is no try.**

Anonymous

**Our greatest glory is not
in never failing,
but in rising every time we fail.**

Confucius

**I am not a product of my circumstances.
I am a product of my decisions.**

Stephen Covey

**Put your heart, mind, and soul
into even your smallest acts.**

This is the secret of success.

Swami Sivananda

**Habit is habit, and not to be flung
out of the window by any man,
but coaxed downstairs
one step at a time.**

Mark Twain

**You miss 100 percent
of the shots you don't take.**

Wayne Gretzky

Great men; great flaws.

The Talmud

"

WE ALL MAKE MISTAKES; TRY TO MAKE NEW ONES.

Noah benShea

**Every strike brings me closer
to the next home run.**

Babe Ruth

Pick up your pieces.

Then, help me gather mine.

Vera Nazarian

**The best time to plant a tree
was twenty years ago.**

The second best time is now.

Chinese Proverb

You are not Humpty Dumpty.

We have all broken something.

Or felt broken.

**Don't confuse feeling broken
with being broken.**

**God is whole, and you are made
in God's image.**

Noah benShea

Pain in this life is not avoidable,

**But the pain we create
avoiding pain is avoidable.**

R. D. Laing

**A problem ignored
is a crisis invented.**

Henry Kissinger

" SOMETIMES NOTHING SO BRINGS US BACK TO LIFE LIKE BEING SCARED TO DEATH.

Noah benShea

**Life is often heavy only because
we attempt to carry it.**

Noah benShea

We're all inventors.

**We all have a hand
inventing our problems.**

Noah benShea

Chapter Ten

EXPLORATION

I gave away my last block of hashish, and at the airport I made a pledge to myself: No more illegal drugs ever. I kept that vow. Unfortunately, it was the drinking that was killing me.

Susanne Johnson

Growing up in Germany, it's very common to vacation in other countries. And it was during a two-week trip to Egypt that I fell in love. I was at a transition point in my career, so I returned home, packed a few duffel bags, and never looked back.

Often, there's a very specific kind of person who lives abroad, especially in a Middle Eastern country. They worked hard and played hard, and it was a party lifestyle. I didn't work, but I enjoyed the parties—at embassies, beaches and private places for any possible occasion.

You had a lot of people hanging out and just drinking. I didn't have to pretend anymore to be a functional alcoholic and get to work on time. Without that restriction, my drinking skyrocketed. Everyone drank. With my alcohol abuse, I finally felt like I fit in.

In Egypt, the rules were completely different. Drugs were illegal, but a lot of the police were smoking hash with me. They were my friends. I was living in a community where there was no negative impact, no drunk driving laws, no ramifications to my substance abuse. Talk about enabling!

Not that my increased alcohol abuse and drug use went unnoticed. I noticed it. My husband noticed. I began having a lot of anxiety issues and panic attacks. The lifestyle was no longer working for me, and I realized I was going to kill myself. It was time to leave the party behind for a fresh start.

I gave away my last block of hashish, and at the airport. Leaving Egypt after 10 years to move to California, I made a pledge to myself: No more illegal drugs ever. I kept that vow. Unfortunately, it was the drinking that was killing me.

I knew I needed help, so I went to my doctor. I wanted to slow down to maybe just one drink a day, one glass of wine at dinner like "normal" people. He told me I had to stop, so I found a different doctor who would say what I wanted to hear. He gave me Xanax to assist me in slowing down my drinking. The bottle read "take as needed," and I did. I had no idea that by doing so I would develop a problem with alcohol and benzodiazepines.

My health deteriorated quickly. Soon I was throwing up blood. My esophagus ruptured and I had an internal bleed out. I could have died, but a week later I came home and started drinking again. It happened three times that year. I was so scared that I had to pick up a glass again every time I came home from the hospital. Then, the last time, I stopped breathing and my heart stopped beating. Boold had to removed from my lungs, and I was on a ventilator. They revived my heart, but when I woke up days later, I was partially paralyzed and didn't know my name. I walked again after a week, with twenty-two rubber bands holding my esophagus together. I was discharged on a clear liquid diet and found myself drinking after just a few days, sitting on the floor, crying.

I had to do something, but I didn't know where to start. I opened up my laptop and randomly found a treatment center called Michael's House. The man who picked up the phone spent four hours with me. I was crying, I had no idea what treatment looked like, but he patiently explained everything, showing me pictures on the computer and booking my flight. I had my last drink at the doorstep of the treatment center.

I had a wrong picture of how an alcoholic looked and what alcohol can do to you. It took me by surprise and almost took my life. I remember telling myself after that ticket was booked, *God must still have plans for me.* And he did. I was lucky I dialed the right number at the right moment, but there are not enough of those people on the other end of the line. So I got into recovery in 2010, was certified as a sober coach in 2013 and an interventionist in 2014, and a recovery specialist in 2016.

I love helping people like I was helped. I can see in the other person the exact same fears and insecurities that I had. Through this work, I've found the "something more" that God had for me. It's why I'm here.

Susanne Johnson

**Because some people once
thought the world was flat**

**Didn't mean Columbus
sailed over the edge.**

All information is not equal.

Noah benShea

**Exploration is really
the essence of the human spirit.**

Frank Borman

**You can never plan the future
by the past.**

Edmund Burke

"

IF YOU'RE LOOKING FOR A WAY OUT OF YOUR PROBLEM, REMEMBER YOU'RE THE ONE WHO FOUND YOUR WAY IN.

Noah benShea

Man cannot discover new oceans,

**Unless he has the courage
to lose sight of the shore.**

André Gide

Aspects of the extraordinary

**Are in every aspect
of the ordinary.**

Noah benShea

**I have found that
every experience is a
form of exploration.**

Ansel Adams

"

WHEN WE SHUT OUR EYES THE WORLD DOES NOT GO INTO HIDING.

Noah benShea

**Live as if you were
to die tomorrow.**

**Learn as if you were
to live forever.**

Mahatma Gandhi

**In the day of prosperity be joyful,
but in the day of adversity consider.**

King Solomon

Set out from any point.

They are all alike.

**They all lead to
a point of departure.**

Antonio Porchia

The path ahead is the way within.

Within you.

**Every line extended far enough
into space curves back on itself.**

Noah benShea

**Emergencies have always been
necessary to progress.**

It was darkness, which produced the lamp.

It was fog that produced the compass.

It was hunger that drove us to exploration.

Victor Hugo

Exploration is not a neat game.

Noah benShea

"

SADNESS IS OFTEN SHADOWING JOY, AND JOY IS OFTEN LURKING IN DEPRESSION.

Noah benShea

**Destiny is a journey
not a destination.**

Noah benShea

Destiny will find you.

**Who destiny finds
is up to you.**

Noah benShea

**Care about what other people
think and you will always
be their prisoner.**

Lao Tzu

"

STOP PLAYING HIDE 'N' SEEK WITH YOURSELF. ALLEY ALLEY OXEN FREE FREE FREE!

Noah benShea

**Fear is always a good
starting point.**

**Find your fears and
you find your work.**

Noah benShea

**If you don't know where you are going,
any road will get you there.**

Lewis Carroll

**The depth of a man is a limit
only he can know . . .**

Kyle Schmalenberg

"

TOO MANY OF US ARE AFRAID TO FIND OUR WAY. BECAUSE WE ARE HESITANT WE WILL FIND OURSELVES ALONG THE WAY.

Noah benShea

**One of the greatest regrets
in life is being what others
would want you to be,**

Rather than being yourself.

Shannon Alder

Before he goes into the water,

**A diver cannot know
what he will bring back.**

Max Ernst

**We all make choices;
in the end our choices make us.**

Ken Levine

To live is to go on a journey;
to die is to come back home.

Put this on a postcard
and send it to yourself.

Anonymous

To grow old is a wonderful thing

If we do not forget
what it is to begin again.

Martin Buber

You are evolving
with or without you.

And you cannot dismiss
what you cannot deny.

Noah benShea

"

TO EXPLORE YOUR LIFE, TO SEE WHO YOU MIGHT YET BECOME, TO LEAVE BEHIND THE LESS IN YOU, IS HEALTH.

Noah benShea

Chapter Eleven

GROWTH

*Gratitude for getting to be a healer
is a miracle in my life.*

Beth Sack

I've been working in the field of drug and alcohol treatment for two decades, finding my way there through a personal experience. When I was sixteen, my dad went into residential treatment for alcoholism. He got into recovery on his first attempt, and I joined in the process. I attended the family program at the center, felt comfortable in that world, and by high school knew I wanted to pursue a degree in counseling.

Of course, learning about addiction was one thing, but working in the field was another. Armed with a master's in addiction sciences, I landed my first job at an outpatient facility outside of Chicago.

Here I was, this little suburban girl, thrown into the deep end. I was given a group to lead, and it was sink or swim. So I began paddling and haven't stopped. An early case was a guy who had just been released from prison for murder.

Looking back, I'm grateful that's where I got my start. Today, I'm the manager of addiction services at Linden Oaks in Illinois. And while my role has changed many times, I always make sure to stay connected to the people.

On Saturday mornings, I get to reconnect with the people we've helped. Seeing those people who've made it gives me so much hope.

I don't think I've ever felt burned out. Even starting out, at twenty-four years old, I felt discouraged at times, but I never felt burned out.

In the last few years, we've seen an increase in heroin and I've been to some funerals and wakes that hit me hard. That's when it's important to go back to those places that remind you of the hope. Sometimes, it requires a little extra self-care.

There are also little miracles that come of out nowhere. We hold an annual 5K run during recovery month, and when someone on the 5K committee stopped by a local coffee shop to ask about the possibility of a sponsorship, the manager said, "Why not," then he said, "Linden Oaks saved my life!"

Miracles happen more often than you think in this line of work. Former patients come up to me all the time and say, "You probably never thought I was going to make it." To see them productive and happy and full of hope is the best feeling in the world. It's an everyday miracle. And gratitude for getting to be a healer is a miracle in my life.

Beth Sack

**Strength is not the
absence of weakness**

**But how we wrestle
with our weaknesses.**

Noah benShea

**Everybody thinks
of changing humanity**

**And nobody thinks
of changing himself.**

Leo Tolstoy

All life is an experiment.

**The more experiments you make
the better.**

Ralph Waldo Emerson

"

LETTING GO IS VERY DIFFERENT FROM GIVING UP.

Noah benShea

**Strength and growth
only come through continuous
effort and struggle.**

Napoleon Hill

**Growth is never
by mere chance.**

**It is the result of forces
working together.**

James Cash Penney

**The great danger for most
of us is not that our aim is
too high and we miss it,**

**But that it is too low
and we reach it.**

Michelangelo

"

LIFE IS AN ORCHARD. EVERY MOMENT IS RIPE WITH OPPORTUNITY.

Noah benShea

**I never found a companion
that was so companionable
as solitude.**

Henry David Thoreau

No one save us but ourselves.

Buddha

**We cannot solve our problems
with the same thinking we used
when we created them.**

Albert Einstein

**Everyone wants to live
on top of the mountain,
but all the happiness and growth
occurs while you're climbing it.**

Anonymous

Life changes when we do.

Noah benShea

**Obstacles are put in our way
to see if what we want
is really worth fighting for.**

Unknown

**Difficulties strengthen the mind,
as labor does the body.**

Seneca

If you would be a real seeker after truth,

**It is necessary that at least
once in your life you doubt,**

As far as possible, all things.

René Decartes

You are not your past mistakes.

To hold that as you is the mistake.

Noah benShea

" DON'T CONFUSE LIVING IN THE FAST LANE WITH BEING STUCK IN THE PAST LANE.

Noah benShea

"

We are products of our past,

But we don't have
to be prisoners of it.

Rick Warren

The only real mistake
is the one from which
we learn nothing.

John Powell

The body grows slowly and steadily
but the soul grows by leaps and bounds.

It may come to its full stature
in an hour.

L. M. Montgomery

**When you are finished changing,
you are finished.**

Benjamin Franklin

**At the center of your being
you have the answer;**

**You know who you are
and you know what you want.**

Lao Tzu

**Do you not see how necessary
a world of pains and troubles is
to school an intelligence . . . ?**

John Keats

"

WE CAN LEARN TO CHANGE IF WE SEE CHANGE AS OUR OPPORTUNITY TO LEARN.

Noah benShea

**The greatest thing in this world
is not so much where we stand
as in what direction we are moving.**

Oliver Wendell Holmes

**Out of your vulnerabilities
will come your strength.**

Sigmund Freud

The world changes when we do.

Anonymous

"

DON'T CONFUSE A LOVE OF POWER WITH THE POWER OF LOVE. ACCESS YOUR POWER BY DARING TO BE LOVING.

Noah benShea

**My destination is no longer a place,
rather a new way of seeing.**

Marcel Proust

**Men do not quit playing
because they grow old;
they grow old because they quit playing.**

Oliver Wendell Holmes

**This life therefore is not righteousness,
but growth in righteousness, not health,
but healing, not being but becoming,
not rest but exercise. We are not yet what we
shall be, but we are growing toward it,
the process is not yet finished,
but it is going on, this is not the end,
but it is the road. All does not yet gleam
in glory, but all is being purified.**

Martin Luther

"

DON'T CONFUSE BEING RIGHT WITH BEING RIGHTEOUS OR BEING WRONGED WITH BEING WRONG.

Noah benShea

**Our fears only have
the power we give them.**

Noah benShea

**Find out what a person
fears most and that is where
he will develop next.**

C. G. Jung

Rocks in my path?

I keep them all.

With them I shall build my castle.

Nemo Nox

FEAR IS THE PAIN BEFORE THE WOUND.

Noah benShea

Anytime you enjoy the
sweet fruits of the tree,
remember the dirty roots of the tree.

Ernest Yeboah

Take a piece of a coal—
a nothing-special rock.

Put it under a lot of pressure
for a long time

And you have a diamond.

And you have a gem—like you!

Noah benShea

Seek out that particular mental attribute
which makes you feel most deeply
and vitally alive, along with which
comes the inner voice which says,
"This is the real me," and when you
have found that attitude, follow it.

William James

For heaven's sake,

Pick up a brush.

Work on your canvas.

Gauguin was a bank teller at forty.

Don't confuse too late with late.

Noah benShea

**Personal growth can simply be
a shift in personal perspective.**

First you look up to yourself.

Then you look down at yourself.

**And finally you must
look at yourself.**

Noah benShea

**Nothing wilts faster than
laurels that have been rested upon.**

Percy Bysshe Shelley

**When Dr. Roger Bannister broke the
four-minute mile, he collapsed,
and because others had told him that to
break the four-minute would kill a man,
he thought he died. Limiting your
expectations for you by the expectations
of others is suicide of the soul.**

Noah benShea

**Our endless and impossible journey
toward home is in fact our home.**

David Foster Wallace

**We become aware
of the void as we fill it.**

Antonio Porchia

" IF YOU KNOW YOUR HABITS ARE BECOMING HANDCUFFS, KNOW YOU ARE ALSO THE KEY.

Noah benShea

For heaven's sake,

Don't let people with muddy emotions

Into your inner space
without taking off their shoes.

Noah benShea

The height of a building
is determined by its foundation.

Noah benShea

We find comfort among
those who agree with us—
growth among those who don't.

Frank Clark

**If you are irritated by every rub,
how will your mirror be polished?**

Rumi

**Someone else's map
can only take you to where
someone else is hoping to go.**

Noah benShea

**Time introduces all of us
to the stranger in the mirror.**

Noah benShea

"

NOTHING EVER BLOSSOMED THAT HADN'T EXPERIENCED BEING COVERED IN DIRT.

Noah benShea

**Love requires us to
take in the stranger,
even if it's our self.**

Noah benShea

**Learning is like rowing upstream;
not to advance is to drop back.**

Proverb

From the cradle to the grave,

**Joy and pain is the
fertilizer for wisdom.**

T. F. Hodge

"

NOTHING IS MADE; EVERYTHING IS RE-MADE FROM WHAT HAS BEEN MADE.

Noah benShea

**All people may have in them
some vocation**

**Which is not quite
plain to themselves . . .**

**They may seem idle and weak
because they are growing.**

**We should be very patient
with each other, I think.**

George Eliot

Being kind makes you kind.

The Dalai Lama

**Commitment is an act,
not a word.**

Jean-Paul Sartre

**Work is about a search for daily meaning
as well as daily bread.**

Studs Terkel

Almost everything will work

**If you unplug for a few minutes,
including you.**

Anne Lamott

**Neurosis is when we
choose to do something**

That is negative but familiar

**Over something,
which is healthy but new.**

Noah benShea

Rivers know this:

There is no hurry.

We shall get there some day.

A. A. Milne

**The number one illness
in the world is depression.**

**The number one reason
for depression is stress.**

**The number one stress is when
people try to be in control of things
that are out of their control.**

**You are not in charge of what
the world delivers to your doorstep.**

You are in charge of your response.

Respond don't react.

Noah benShea

**There is no adversity
that cannot bear a gift**

**And no gift that cannot
bring adversity.**

Mollie Marti

**Knowing yourself is
the beginning of all wisdom.**

Aristotle

**The young fear change
will never come.**

The old fear it will.

Fears change when we do.

Noah benShea

PERSONAL GROWTH IS ALWAYS PERSONAL.

Noah benShea

Don't base your decision

**On the opinions of those
who don't want to see you grow.**

Yvonne Pierre

Growth is not a polite visitor.

Noah benShea

**Every private deceit
will eventually become
a public deceit.**

Noah benShea

"

THOSE WHO FEAR TO GROW WILL ALSO BE AFRAID THAT YOU WILL.

Noah benShea

**Every great adventure
begins with a farewell.**

Ron Koslow

**What grows
never grows old.**

Noah benShea

And After All the Wisdom

THERE IS THIS . . .

"Jacob," said the children, "tell us a story!"

"The number one illness in the world," said Jacob, "is depression.

"The number one reason for depression is stress.

"And the number one stress is people trying to control what they cannot control."

"The lesson?" asked Samuel, his eyes riveted on Jacob.

"We are not in charge of what the world delivers to our door," said Jacob.

"We are in charge of our response."

"And the challenge?"

"The challenge," said Jacob, "is to respond, not react."

"But," said Samuel, "doesn't stress weigh heavily on all of us?"

"Stress," said Jacob, "only has the weight we give it."

"I don't understand," said Samuel. "Surely we have all seen the burden of stress in life."

"Imagine stress was a glass of water," said Jacob. "To lift the glass is not a burden. But, the longer we were required to hold the glass up, the heavier it becomes. The glass's weight after five minutes would be far different than the torture to hold it up for five hours, or five years."

"So?"

"So," said Jacob, "stress's weight, and its burden in our lives, is solely conditioned by how long we hold onto our stress."

"So for the stress in our life to weigh less, we have to . . . "

"Let go of our commitment to hold onto our stress," said Jacob.

"And to lift our spirits?"

"And to lift our spirits," said Jacob, "we only have to stop doing what is bringing us down."

Noah benShea
Author of Jacob's Children

Faith

Courage

Honesty

Forgiveness

Growth

Inspiration

Renewal

Empowerment

Hope

Biographies and Photos of Contributors

Beth Sack

Beth Sack is the manager of addiction services at Linden Oaks Behavioral Health in Naperville, Illinois. Knowing what she wanted to do from an early age, Beth earned a masters degree in addiction sciences and immediately began working in the treatment field. She has spent her entire career—two decades—helping those in need of addiction and mental health services.

Brian O'Shea

Brian O'Shea is the founder of the Jackson, Mississippi-based company Caring Interventions, opened in 2009, but his experience with interventions dates back much earlier than that. He serves as the company's lead interventionist and sober coach. The opportunity to offer to others the hope he's found is what gets him out of bed each morning.

Darren Kavinoky

Darren is the founder of 1-800-N-O-C-U-F-F-S (662-8337) and the Kavinoky Law Firm. He's also an accomplished trial lawyer, a well-known television host, and a sought after legal analyst and public speaker. He's appeared on *Today*, *The View*, *Entertainment Tonight*, *The Insider*, *Dr. Phil*, *Dr. Drew*, CNN, HLN, Fox News, and countless other TV and radio shows.

John Southworth

A Certified Alcohol and Drug Counselor and Board Registered Interventionist, John Southworth founded Southworth Associates International in 1998. Based in Boise, Idaho, the company provides interventions, consulting, and monitoring services worldwide. The year 2014 marked John's thirtieth year as an interventionist. In that time, he's conducted hundreds of successful interventions, both nationally and internationally, on a professional and public level.

Judith Landau

A global addiction and trauma pioneer, Judith Landau is president and CEO of ARISE and the codeveloper of the evidence-based, best practice ARISE® Continuum of Care. Dr. Landau is also a child, family, and community neuropsychiatrist, former professor of psychiatry and family medicine, and an isangoma or traditional African healer.

Matthew Read

Matthew has been a flight attendant for twenty-four years and has been part of the Flight Attendant Drug and Alcohol Program (FADAP), regularly attending annual conferences. He's also a passionate speaker on the topic of recovery. He is based in Philadelphia for work, but he makes his home bear Orlando, Florida, where he lives with his loving partner of eight years.

Heidi Huerta

Heidi Huerta joined the staff of Heroes in Recovery in 2013 as the organization's community manager. She is also an avid runner and yogi, finding community on the roads and on her mat. Originally from Pensacola, Florida and educated in Westchester County, New York, Heidi's journey has brought her to Nashville, Tennessee, where she lives with her Chihuahua, Buddy.

Tondra Frisby

Tondra K. Frisby established S.T.E.P. Intervention Services in 2007. Being in recovery since 1996, she has a deep passion and desire to help those suffering from the disease of addiction to get into treatment, while also providing education, resources, and comfort for the entire family.

Susanne Johnson

Originally from Germany, Susanne Johnson has traveled the world, living on three continents and visiting nearly fifty countries. Susanne is a certified sober coach, certified interventionist, and certified recovery specialist. She has been a lead advocate with Heroes in Recovery since 2012. She moved to the U.S. in 2006 and currently resides in the small community of Metropolis, Illinois, with her American-born husband.

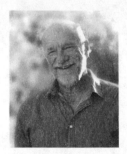

Noah benShea

Noah benShea is one of North America's most respected and beloved poet philosophers. He is international best selling author of 25 books translated into 18 languages. Has spoken at the Library of Congress, been nominated for The Pulitzer Prize, and was the subject of a National Public Television Special. He is the Executive Director of The Justice Project and is The National Philosopher for Foundations Recovery Network.

For more information, please visit: www.NoahbenShea.com.